HE AND SHE

OR

A POET'S PORTFOLIO

BY

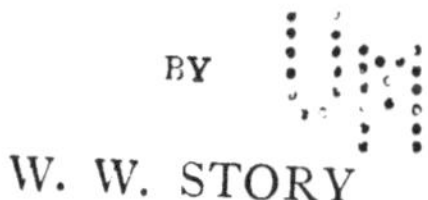

W. W. STORY

BOSTON AND NEW YORK
HOUGHTON, MIFFLIN AND COMPANY
The Riverside Press, Cambridge
1894

EIGHTEENTH EDITION.

The Riverside Press, Cambridge, Mass., U. S. A.
Printed by H. O. Houghton & Company.

HE AND SHE;

OR, A POET'S PORTFOLIO.

He was in the habit of wandering alone, during the summer mornings, through the forest and along the mountain side, and one of his favorite haunts was a picturesque glen, where he often sat for hours alone with nature, lost in vague contemplation: now watching the busy insect life in the grass or in the air; now listening to the chirruping of birds in the woods, the murmuring of bees hovering about the flowers, or the welling of the clear mountain torrent, that told forever its endless tale as it wandered by mossy boulders and rounded stones down to the valley below; now gazing idly into the sky, against which the overhanging beeches printed their leaves in tessellated light and dark, or vaguely watching the lazy clouds that trailed across the tender blue; now noting in his portfolio some passing thought, or fancy, or feeling, that threw its gleam of light or shadow across his dreaming mind.

Here, leaning against one of the mossy boulders, in the shadow of the beeches, he was writing in his portfolio one summer morning, when she accidentally found him, and the following conversation took place:—

She. Ah, here you are, sitting under this old beech and scribbling verses, as usual, are you not? Why don't you rest and lie fallow? You are always working your brains. All work and no play—and you know the rest. Come, confess!

He. I confess, I can't help it.

She. You can if you choose.

He. But suppose I don't choose; suppose it is my delight to do this. Nature is always teasing me to do something for her,—to dress her in verse, or in some shape or other of art; and she has such subtle powers of persuasion that I cannot resist her. You know that in some ways you are her child, and I doubt if I could refuse you anything.

She. Well, I take you at your word. Read me what you have written.

He. It is only rubbish; it is scarce worth your hearing.

She. Let me be the judge. You have, I see, a book full of what you call rubbish. You have promised me so often to read me some of your poems, and the time has now come to fulfill your promise. Don't be shy. You know you want to read them to me. There never was a poet who did not like to read his verses.

He. Not to everybody.

She. Ah, then, you don't think me worthy to hear them.

He. No; I don't think them worthy to be heard by you.

She. Nonsense! You like to read them; I like to hear them. Here we are in this delightful glen; there is no one near to interrupt us; we have the whole day before us; I have a piece of embroidery to occupy my hands; and I will promise to praise every poem you read.

He. Then I won't read you a word of anything I have here.

She. Oh, yes, you will. You know you wish me to praise them. What poet was ever willing to read his verses unless he expected or at least hoped to be praised? You cannot pretend you wish me to criticise them and find fault with them.

He. But I do; that is just what I should like. I should like to have an honest opinion, if I ever could get it; but that is of all things the most difficult tc obtain from any one. We always have either a friend who overpraises, or a critic who undervalues, or a brother-poet whose personality interferes with his judgment, or an indifferent person who does not take interest enough to have an opinion, or some one who is kneaded up of prose, and sees no reason for singing clothes, or — a fool.

She. And in the last class are all, I suppose, who think your verses are poor stuff?

He. I dare say there is something in that, and they may be right in their opinion, but of course we don't like it.

She. Well, I don't come under any class you have mentioned, and I insist on hearing some of these verses.

He. And you will be honest with me?

She. As honest as I dare to be with a poet who reads me his poems. Now begin.

He. But really, I assure you, I have nothing here worth your listening to. This is only a book where I carelessly jot down whatever comes into my head just as it comes. It is full of first sketches, half-finished things, glimpses of thoughts or feelings or persons. They are not really poems. That is too high and honorable a name to give them.

She. Ah, but that is just what I like to hear. It will be like looking over an artist's sketch-book, where things are half done, just begun, altered, erased, outlined, unframed, and these always have a peculiar charm that finished work never has; a freshness and careless grace that elaboration tames and spoils. Ah! read me these. They let one into the secret laboratory of the poet's mind.

He. Or behind the scenes, where the machinery is visible, and everything is rude and rough and out of place.

She. Well, there is a fascination in that, too. There is where the friends of the actors and authors are permitted to go. But begin: time is flying, the day is passing.

He. Ah, yes, if we only could stop Time when all is happy and bright! But then it swiftest flees away. Here, listen, since you will hear something. This is apropos.

O beloved day,
Stay with us, oh stay!
Hurry not with cruel haste thus so swift away.

All is now so fair;
Love is in the air;
More than this of happiness scarce the heart could bear.

Nothing short of heaven,
That perhaps not even
Sweeter, dearer, more divine, will to us be given.

Dearest, on my breast
Lean thy head and rest:
Nothing that this world can give is better; this is best.

Life is in its prime,
And the glad springtime
Breathes its subtle odors through us, turning thought to rhyme.

To its very rim
Joy life's cup doth brim ;
Nature, smiling all around us, sings its happy hymn.

Love its perfect tune
On the harp of June
Plays the while the whole world listens, 'neath the pulsing noon.

Almost 't is a pain
In the heart and brain ;
All the nerves of life are thrilling with its rapturous strain.

Stay with us, oh, stay,
Dear, beloved day !
Flower and bloom of full creation, never pass away.

There, I read it to you just as I wrote it, without a correction, since you will have sketches.

She. It is what I call a rapturous sigh for the impossible. And the beloved one ? — but I must not ask who she was.

He. Oh, yes ; you may. She was a most exquisite creature. You never knew her ; nor I either.

She. Well, that is some satisfaction. She was not real.

He. Oh yes, perfectly real ; more real than any actual person I know. But with the day and the hour she vanished, like the weird sisters of Macbeth, into air.

She. It must have been a charming day to have inspired such verses. That, at all events, must have been a fact.

He. Certainly. The day was a fact. Here is the date, November 21, and a note in my diary, " Rains cats and dogs and pitchforks, and I think the wind is mad ; it blows so that the whole house shudders." You see, I made the day as well as the person and the poem.

She. There is no believing anything that poets say. I suppose had it been a faultless day in June, you would have been mooning and moaning over somebody and something.

He. Ah, but all days do not turn out

just as this did. Our beautiful days are those we don't expect, which fall to us out of heaven, perfect and with a sweet surprise. Others to which we have looked forward, and from which we have expected so much — too much — are so often only disappointments. We profess to enjoy them, but we do not; they are failures. We cannot hunt joy into its fastnesses; it flies before the hunter, and comes suddenly forward to meet us face to face when we least look for it. Some of our beautiful days turn out, for instance, like this: —

Yes, 't was a beautiful day,
The guests were all laughing and gay;
All said they enjoyed and admired.
But oh, I 'm so tired, — so tired!
I 'm glad that the night 's coming on,
I am glad to get home and be quiet;
I am glad that the long day is done,
With its noise and its laughter and riot.

For somehow, it seemed like a fate,
I was always a moment too late:
The music just stopped when I came,
I saw but the fireworks' last flame;

The dancing was over, the dancers
Were laughing and going away ;
The curtain had dropped, and the foot-
lights
Were all that I saw of the play.

It was only my luck, I suppose ;
And the day was delightful to those
Who were right in their time and their
place.
But for me, I did nothing but race
And struggle ; and all was in vain.
We cannot have all of us prizes,
And a pleasure that 's missed is a pain,
And one balance goes down as one rises.

And I 'm tired, — so tired at last
That I 'm glad that the great day is past.
The pleasure I sought for I missed,
And I ask, Did it really exist ?
Were they happy who smiled so, and said
'T was delightful, exciting, enchanting ?
I doubt it ; but they perhaps had
Just the something I always was wanting.

In the triumph, I ask, does the crown
Never crease the smooth brow to a frown ?
Does the wine that our spirits makes gay

Leave the head free from aches the next
day ?
Is the joy, when 't is caught, worth the
while
Of the struggle and labor to win it ?
Has love a perpetual smile,
And life's best no bitterness in it ?

It may be, and yet at its best,
When the wave of life towers to its crest,
Ere its rim for a moment can flash
In its joy-light, it breaks with a crash,
And shattered sinks down on the shore ;
For the strength of desire has departed,
The glory and gladness are o'er,
And it dies in despair, broken-hearted.

She. Life is just such a day.

He. Ah yes, but too often.

She. If we could only be content with what we have, how much happier we should be. But the hope that beckons us into the future commonly spoils the present. The music is always on the next field ; the promise is always sweeter than the performance ; we are always either looking back and regretting, or looking forward and hoping, and the actual present, which stands offering us flowers, we treat with scorn, or at least with indifference. The gods have eternally the present; for them is no future, no past; and so they are divine. It is only Satan who tempts us with the future, or taunts us with the past, because we are mortals; and thus he jeers at us, and spoils all we really own. Joy is only a dream.

He. But a dream is not always a joy. Here, for instance, is one if you would like to hear it; whether from the ivory gate or not, you shall say. But before I read this dream, since I have given you two Days, let me now give you one Night, the end of all the banquet, and the dancing, and the laughter: —

Through the casement the wind is moaning,
  On the pane the ivy crawls;
The fire is faded to ashes,
  And the black brand broken falls.

The voices are gone, but I linger,
  And silence is over all;
Where once there was music and laughter
  Stands Death in the empty hall.

There is only a dead rose lying
  Faded and crushed on the floor,
And a harp whose strings are broken,
  That Love will play no more.

She. Oh, too, too sad; I am sorry you read it.

He. Well, life is so.

She. I don't care if it is, one should not dwell on it. Now for the dream. Was it a real one ?

He. Yes, a real one; and you will see what a pleasant one it was.

Last night I had a tiger to play with,
  Ah yes, as you say, 't was only a dream,
But even in a dream to play with a tiger
  Is not so pleasant as it may seem.

She was smooth and supple, and lithe and graceful,
  But she watched me with ever flashing eye.
And I felt forever a horrible feeling
  While that tiger was with me, that death was nigh;

That at any moment her claws might rend me,
And an instant's passion might cost me my life.
So I gave her whatever she wanted to soothe her,
And promised to make this tiger my wife.

But what was curious — though in dreaming,
There is nothing that really does surprise —
Was that it seemed to be you, dear Annie,
And had your graces, and had your eyes.

She. Oh, that is really unpardonable. Who was it that refused you a turn in the waltz, or would not pin a cotillion favor on your coat, that you thus revenged yourself upon her? Annie — Annie — Who was Annie?

He. You always want to know the unknowable. You always suppose that such verses apply to an individual.

She. Yes, they always have a root in some fact or person. They are not all made out of your brain; they are not wholly fictions. You need not pretend that they are.

He. I do not. But one imagines all sorts of things that are false, and I confess that I amuse myself often in society, by looking into the windows of persons I do not know to see what they are about within.

She. Looking in at windows! I am ashamed of you.

He. The windows I mean are the eyes. Strange creatures look through them — tigers, lambs, devils, angels.

She. Oh! well. I am glad to hear that there are angels sometimes. Thank you. I was afraid you only saw wild beasts in our eyes.

He. Sometimes tenderness infinite, oftener devils of jealousy and hatred, and very frequently empty rooms, with not even a little devil in them, much less an angel. We get strange peeps at times into the world within, when we least expect it.

She. So it was not because Annie would not give you a waltz?

He. No. I told you 't was a real

dream. This is my idea of a waltz, when Annie gives me one : —

My arm is around your waist, love,
  Your hand is clasping mine,
Your head leans over my shoulder,
  As around in the waltz we twine.
I feel your quick heart throbbing,
  Your panting breath I breathe,
And the odor rare of your hyacinth hair
  Comes faintly up from beneath.

To the rhythmic beat of the music,
  In the floating ebb and flow
Of the tense violin, and the lisping flute,
  And the burring bass we go.
Whirling, whirling, whirling,
  In a rapture swift and sweet,
To the pleading violoncello's tones,
  And the pulsing piano's beat.

The world is alive with motion,
  The lights are whirling all,
And the feet and brain are stirred by the
    strain
  Of the music's incessant call.
Dance ! dance ! dance ! it calls to us ;
  And borne on the waves of sound,

We circling swing, in a dizzy ring,
  With the whole world wheeling round.

The jewels dance on your bosom,
  On your arms the bracelets dance,
The swift blood speaks in your mantling
      cheeks,
  In your eyes is a dewy trance ;
Your white robes flutter around you,
  Nothing is calm or still,
And the senses stir in the music's whirr
  With a swift electric thrill.

We pause ; and your waist releasing,
  We stand and breathe for a while ;
And, your face afire with a sweet desire,
  You look in my eyes and smile.
We scarcely can speak for panting,
  But I lean to you, and say,
Ah ! who, my love, can resist you,
  You have waltzed my heart away.

She. It gets into my feet as well as my head, this waltz of yours.

He. The lines have perhaps a certain kind of movement in them, defective as they are ; but they were scribbled in a corner of a ball-room while waltzers were whirling dizzily round, and the lights were shaking and the music was going; so you cannot expect they should have any thing more than mere go.

She. Mere go! You speak of that as if it were nothing; but after all, is not that the secret of a good deal of our poetry, and especially that of Byron? You cannot look into it with a critical eye. It is full of bad English, and false metaphor, and strained sentiment; but there is "go" in it, and it intoxicates the thoughts and senses, so that one ceases to be critical. *Glissez, glissez mortels, n'appuyez pas,* should be your rule in reading him. It won't do to linger. You must gulp, not sip.

He. At all events, he did not overrefine as some of our modern poets do. For instance, there is ——, I suppose he means something, but his meaning is so involved in a complicated web of vague and far-fetched words and phrases, that sometimes it is not a little difficult to get at it; and I am not sure that after you have got at it, it is worth the trouble.

She. No, we are now getting so euphuistic, that I don't pretend to understand half I read, though I am a woman, and much of it, apparently, is written specially for us women; or at least so it would seem, there is so little that is manly in it.

He. Some of them talk like Hamlet's friend, Osric — "after what flourish their natures will." Here is a profile sketch of ——. Do you recognize it?

She. Oh, very like; and what are the lines you have written under it?

He. Mere nonsense.

She. Read them.

He.

A Brahmin he sits apart,
Our modern poet, and gazes
Attentively into his heart,
And its faint and vaporous phases,
Examines with infinite care.
All his feelings are thin as air,
All his passions are mild as milk.
He loves but the quaint and the old,
He dares not be simple and bold,
But refines and refines and refines,
And treads on a thread as spare
As the spider's gauzy silk,
That trembles in all its lines

With the breeze, and can scarcely hold
The dewdrop the morning has strung ;
And so 'twixt the earth and the sky,
And to neither wed, he is hung ;
And he ponders his words and his rhymes,
And his delicate tinkle of chimes,
And strives to be deep and intense ;
While the world of beauty and sense,
The strong and palpitant world,
The powers and passions of man,
By which it is whipped and whirled,
Are only to him an offense.
'T is the chaff blown away by the fan,
That he gathers his garners to fill,
Not the grain that the world's great mill
Takes out of life as its toll.
For he scorns the common and rude,
And only examines his soul, —
His particular soul, — and wears
A vestment of whims, and of airs,
And of fancies so frail and so thin
That they scarcely can cover the nude.
Little thought he is nursing within,
So sitting alone and apart,
He broods and he broods and he broods,
And plays on his little lute,
And sings of his little moods,
With a sweet æsthetic art,
And his song is —

There, you see, I have left off. What is his song?

She. I suppose it is a ballade, with skim-milk love and fine-drawn sentiment, belonging to some other century, and sung perhaps by a mediæval knight to the accompaniment of some queer instrument, now unknown except in museums, while around him are lying long, lean, languid ladies on a lawn.

He. Charming alliteration, worthy of the theme, but the ballade must have a refrain.

She. Of course, what is a ballade without a refrain?

He. And the refrain must have no connection, as far as meaning goes, with the ballade.

She. Of course not! For whom do you take me, to imagine that I suppose it necessary for a refrain to have any sense? A refrain is always the burden of a poem, and is fitly named a burden.

He. The burden, or bourdon, as Spenser more properly spells it, is intelligible enough in the old ballades, which were at first improvised, or supposed to be improvised, and always were sung or chanted;

and then it represented the pause or rest which the accompanying instrument filled up with its little ritornello, and bourdonned sometimes alone without words, and sometimes with catch-words constantly repeated, so as to give time to the improvisator to think out the following lines, or to the singer to rest his voice or revive his memory. In Italy, as you know, the improvisator is always accompanied by a guitar and mandoline, which *bourdonnent* their little phrase between the lines or the stanzas, and fill up the gaps. But in serious poems of the present day, written to be read and not sung, this repetition of the bourdon without the song is a stumbling block and an offense, and often a mere affectation.

She. None the less Shakespeare uses it.

He. I know he does, here and there in his sonnets, but they were to be sung, not read; for instance, —

"Sing hey, ho, the wind and the rain,
For the rain it raineth every day."

There is a certain grace about that, I admit. But he knew how and when to use it. Nowadays these bourdons bore me, in our modern poems. Suppose, for instance, I should insist in some passionate and pathetic poem in tripping up the reader constantly by interpolating such a refrain as this, —

> The world is wide, the wind is cold,
> Ah me, the new, ah me, the old.

She. There is too much meaning in it. It is not a success as a refrain. It is not so good as your description of the Brahmin poet, wherein, indeed, "his definement suffers no perdition in you."

He. Ah, I see you "know this water-fly," our friend Osric, as Hamlet jeeringly calls him. Let me see — how does he go on, "In the verity of extolment, I take him to be a soul of great article; and his infusion of such dearth and rareness, as, to make true diction of him, his semblable is his mirror."

She. "Your lordship speaks most infallibly of him." Oh, what fun Shakespeare is!

He. Ah, is n't he? I know not which most surprises me in him, his humor or power of passion.

She. Oh, don't let us talk of Shakespeare. If you do I shall hear no more of your verses.

He. What a loss!

She. When we don't get what we want, it is always a loss, whether it is a kingdom or an onion. You need not fish for compliments from me. I promised you to be honest.

He. When one promises to be honest, one means to be severe.

She. Oh, that is your notion of it, is it? and perhaps there is some truth in it. But you have promised to amuse me, so now read me something more, something silly, if you can deign to be silly.

He. Ah, that is cruel. I pride myself on my silliness. Shakespeare, I am sure, was silly; in fact, Ben Jonson, or was it Fuller, as much as tells us so, *aliquid sufflimanandus erat.* He had to be suppressed.

She. There you are back on Shakespeare again. Read your verses and don't talk about him now.

He. In a minute; but first let me read these two sonnets about our great poets.

Whose are those forms august that, in the
press
And busy blames and praises of to-day,
Stand so serene above life's fierce affray
With ever youthful strength and loveli-
ness ?
Those are the mighty makers, whom no
stress
Of time can shame, nor fashion sweep
away,
Whom art begot on nature in the play
Of healthy passion, scorning base excess.
Rising perchance in mists, and half ob-
scure
When up the horizon of their age they
came,
Brighter with years they shine in steadier
light,
Great constellations that will aye en-
dure,
Though myriad meteors of ephemeral
fame
Across them flash, to vanish into night.

Such was our Chaucer in the early prime
Of English verse, who held to Nature's
hand
And walked serenely through its morning
land.

Gladsome and hale, brushing its dewy
rime.
And such was Shakespeare, whose strong
soul could climb
Steeps of sheer terror, sound the ocean
grand
Of passion's deeps, or over Fancy's
strand
Trip with his fairies, keeping step and
time.
His, too, the power to laugh out full and
clear,
With unembittered joyance, and to move
Along the silent, shadowy paths of love
As tenderly as Dante, whose austere,
Stern spirit through the worlds below,
above,
Unsmiling strode, to tell their tidings
here.

She. Very good. Yes, I am glad I did not drive you away from Shakespeare; though when you get on this theme you never come to an end, and I was afraid —

He. He never came to an end.

She. You have said quite enough about him in your two sonnets. And you must give me a copy of them to think over at my leisure. Will you?

He. I am only too happy that you should think them worth having.

She. Well, I do. Now for some silly verses.

He. Here are some silly lines I once wrote at the request of a friend, as an autograph (they even ask autographs from me now, — don't laugh) for a young girl whose very name was unknown to me. "Pray give me your autograph for a dear little friend of mine," she wrote, and I sent her this: —

Oh lovely Annie or,
Jenny, or Fanny, or
Lily, or Bessie, for whom youths are raving,
Love while your youth you own,
For let the truth be known,
Nothing in old age is half worth the having.

She. How do you know?

He. I guess; one is never so old as when one is young.

She. Nor so young as when one is old, perhaps, sometimes. But go on.

Then all regretting
But never forgetting,
Longing for that which has vanished away,
Life creeps on wearily,
Ah ! we cry drearily,
Would I were young again, careless and gay !

She. As if one ever were really — but as if one ever really — but no matter — but no matter; go on.

But when the hair is gray,
When the teeth fall away,
Loving and kissing we lay on life's shelves;
Old age in others is
Charming, in mothers is
Lovely, but somehow 't is not in ourselves.

Talk not to me of fame,
'T is but to be a name,
'T is an old story, that tires when 't is told.
Careless and happy,
Not hairless and cappy,
Love me, my darling, before you grow old.

She. You call that silly? In my opinion it 's the wisest thing you have yet read. Was not your young friend pleased?

He. I don't know. She never told me. She "let concealment like a worm i' the bud feed on her damask cheek." Whether "she sat like patience on a monument smiling at grief" after receiving it, I cannot say. I like to be accurate in these matters, and as far as concealment goes I am sure, but about the monument I am doubtful.

She. I should have been more grateful, but it is so difficult to give expression to one's feelings. I suppose she was afraid to write to you.

He. No doubt I am a terrible person, And I don't wonder she feared me; it gratified my pride. I extend my hand and bless her like a — what shall we say, father, or uncle?

She. Uncle, I think, is best; unless that involves leaving her a fortune. The relation is perilous, one expects a great deal from one's uncle. On the whole, perhaps you had better stick to "friend." That means so much, and then again so little.

He. There is something so patronizing in calling any one your young friend. It assumes such a superiority that my modesty shrinks from it.

She. Ay, but call yourself her old friend; and what a difference! Now, I am your old friend.

He. Yes, so you are, considering —

She. Considering what?

He. Considering that you are still so young.

She. I suppose it never occurred to you to write anything for me.

He. Will you take this?

Little we know what secret influence
A word, a glance, a casual tone may
bring,
That, like the wind's breath on a chorded
string,
May thrill the memory, touch the inner
sense,
And waken dreams that come we know
not whence;
Or like the light touch of a bird's swift
wing,
The lake's still face a moment visiting,
Leave pulsing rings, when he has vanished thence.

You looked into my eyes an instant's
space,
And all the boundaries of time and place
Broke down, and far into a world beyond
Of buried hopes and dreams my soul had
sight,
Where dim desires long lost, and memories fond,
Rose in a soft mirage of tender light.

She. Ah, you never wrote that to me.

He. I might have written it to you, and it is all the same as if I did. It is yours now.

She. I accept it, and thank you. Oh, how true it is that a glance, a word, an inflection of voice, will sometimes carry the spirit so far, far away, and break down all the barriers of the present, and evoke dim memories of the past long buried out of sight! How little we know what secret unconscious influences we exert! We are for the most part islands; spiritual islands, to which no other soul can really reach save by a tone or a glance.

He. And never do we feel this more than in our deep sorrows. Then how terribly far we are from every one; how isolated; how alone. No one can help us then. And equally in our love. Intimate and intense as it may be, the lover and the loved are always two. Their two spirits can no more intermingle than their bodies can. Stop! I have some verses here, somewhere, apropos to this. Ah, here they are.

Thy lips touched mine, there flashed a
 sudden fire
 From brain to brain;
Oh, was it joy, or did that wild desire
 Turn it to pain?

The thirst of soul Love's rapture could
 not slake
 While we were twain;
Of our two beings, one we could not
 make,
 And that was pain.

She. You have not quite succeeded in that poem.

He. No, I know it. It is not what it ought to be, and nothing on earth is; but you know I am not professing to read you poems, but only scraps and sketches, and not because I think them worth much, but because you asked me to read them.

She. You see, I am honest with you. Your idea is good, but you might express it better. It is worth trying for again.

He. Perhaps; but ideas come and go, and if one does not seize them at once they are gone, and they never come back with the same freshness and accidentality. They come and sing a little song to us, and sometimes we hear it right and sometimes wrong; and there is no more virtue in us, if we do not catch it right at first; or, to use another metaphor, if we break a flower when we pluck it, we cannot mend it again. Accident, Fate, Fortune, anything you please, throws us at times her ball, and we either catch it, or we do not. If we do not —

She. We make a mis-take.

He. Is that a pun ?

She. I did not mean it for one, but simply for an analysis of the word, as holding a philosophical truth.

He. As far as life is concerned, everything seems in that sense to be a mistake. But here is another kind of a mistake, which may amuse you.

How your sweet face revives again
The dear old time, my Pearl, —
If I may use the pretty name,
I called you when a girl.

You are so young; while Time of me
Has made a cruel prey,
It has forgotten you, nor swept
One grace of youth away.

The same sweet face, the same sweet smile,
The same lithe figure, too! —
What did you say? "It was perchance
Your mother that I knew?"

Ah, yes, of course, it must have been,
And yet the same you seem,
And for a moment, all these years
Fled from me like a dream.

Then what your mother would not give,
Permit me, dear, to take,
The old man's privilege — a kiss —
Just for your mother's sake.

She. Ha, ha! That was a pretty mistake; but you got out of it fairly well.

He. Yes; I got the old man's privilege, but I don't know that that is a great consolation. A man begins to feel old, really, when the young girls are not shy of him, and let him kiss them without making any fuss about it, but almost as a matter of course. As long as they blush and draw back, he flatters himself that he is not really so old after all. The last, worst phase is when they don't wait for him, but come and kiss him of their own accord. Oh, that is too much. Gout is nothing to that, nor white hairs.

She. Yes, I see; this last kiss is different from the one in the former poem.

He. Rather! There are as many kinds of kisses as of characters. The most foolish of all kisses is that formality between women, who go through the ceremony of rubbing their noses against each other's cheeks and calling it a kiss.

She. Persons who are constantly kissing and calling everybody dear are my aversion. A kiss should really mean something, and when everybody is dear, nobody is. For instance, there is our friend ——, who is so full of tender demonstrations, and never speaks of anybody without an endearing epithet, and who really is a totally neutral being, without color or real feeling or possibility of passion, and who squanders her epithets and kisses for just what they are worth, — nothing. And yet she is perfectly good-natured.

He. Ah, yes, good-natured. Universally good-natured persons are generally shallow and heartless.

She. Oh! no, no. That is going too far.

He. Perhaps; there are exceptions, I dare say. But those gay, bright, sunny little bodies that sparkle along in life, and are always laughing and always gay, are, for the most part, like running streams, — the shallower they are, the greater noise and babble they make. Rivers sweep on calmly and deeply.

She. Don't be led astray by a metaphor. They are dangerous things. They often confuse the judgment by keeping it fixed on two things at once. The illustration blinds the eye to the thing illustrated.

He. But all speech is metaphor.

She. And all speech is dangerous. Silence is golden, speech is silvern.

He. I wish we could keep that word silvern. We say brazen, golden, cedarn, and ought to say silvern. It is the true old English word. And so is eyen for eyes, as we say oxen not oxes. We have already too many final *s's* in our English plurals. But to go back to what we were saying, I don't seriously care for merely good-natured people. I prefer those who are varied in feeling and stiller of nature and stronger of character. I could not love the gay-hearted creature who would bury you without a tear.

She. But why, why should there be any necessary inconsistency between good nature and deep feeling?

He. I don't know why, I merely state the fact. As far as my experience goes, I have so found it.

She. All things are good in their place. The gay, good-natured people lend life to society, and sunshine to home. It would be dismal to have society composed only of people with deep feelings, and perhaps even you will admit that at home there is nothing more delightful than a bright sunny nature, which sees good in all.

He. I give it up. I won't argue with

you, but you know what I mean; and I repeat, those that love everybody love nobody.

She. There are all sorts of tastes; and all sorts of persons are required to make up a world.

He. There are prickly thistles, and bright-eyed daisies, and stately scentless camellias; and there is the rose, — I prefer the rose. And here is a "copy of verses," as our fathers called them, on this subject.

When Nature had shaped her rustic beauties, —
The bright-eyed daisy, the violet sweet,
The blushing poppy that nods and trembles
In its scarlet hood among the wheat, —

She paused and pondered; — and then she fashioned
The scentless camellia proud and cold,
The spicy carnation freaked with passion,
The lily pale for an angel to hold.

All were fair, yet something was wanting,
Of freer perfection, of larger repose;

And again she paused, — then in one glad moment
 She breathed her whole soul into the rose.

With you, dear Violet, Daisy, and Poppy,
 Pleasant it was in the fields to play,
In the careless and heartless joy of childhood,
 When an hour was as long as manhood's day.

And with you, O passionate, bright Carnation,
 A boy's brief love for a time I knew,
And you I admired proud Lady Camellia,
 And, Lily, I sang in the church with you.

But O my Rose, my frank, free-hearted,
 My perfect above all conscious arts,
What were they beside thee, O Rose, my darling,
 To you I have given my heart of hearts.

She. That is pretty; I like that. You might illustrate it with so many pretty drawings.

He. Will you do it?

She. I am afraid I should not be able. But I can see so many pictures one might make, that if nobody else will do it, I will try my hand. And first I will make the children, Poppy, Daisy, and Violet, playing in the garden together, and then the romantic flirtation of Carnation and her young lover in the wood. And then the dance with Lady Camellia, her own white flower in her hair, and he talking to her half-hidden behind a curtain; and then the hymn in the church with Lily. And then, oh then, Rose; and where shall we place her? On a beautiful, smooth-shaven English lawn, sitting or strolling beneath the shadow of the perfumed limes in early summer morning, when the nightingale sings in the trees, and the little birds are hopping along the greensward, and the breeze is rustling in the dewy leaves? Or shall it be at twilight in some shadowy lane, when the eglantine wavers out, spotting with its delicate blossoms the hawthorn hedges, and the rose-clouds are hanging over the sunken sun, and the daffodil sky in the west is paling into soft grays, while in the east the low full moon is softly burning through the distant woods? Or shall they both be sitting by a window, looking out over a sweet, far landscape, with snowy curtains waving in the breath of the June air, and a vase of roses near by scenting the atmosphere? Say, which shall it be?

He. Any, or all. That would be like making music for my words, embalming them, enchanting them, giving them the life and beauty they want, clothing their nakedness with singing robes, till all the world should listen and give the words the charm that the singing only owns. Will you do this?

She. I will try.

He. I shall hold you to your promise, but I know you never will perform it.

She. I only said I would try.

He. And now I will give you another picture to paint for me. It is towards twilight, and two lovers are in a boat; silent, alone, dreaming, their oars suspended; and he leans forward and gazes at her, and she is looking over the side of the boat into the waters, in which the shadows of the trees on the banks and the golden clouds in the sky are softly reflected.

Afloat on the brim of a placid stream,
Pleasant it is to lie and dream,
With heaven above, and far below
The deeps of death — sad deeps that know
The still reflections of earth and sky
In their silent, serene obscurity.
And hanging thus upon Life's thin rim,
Death seems so sweet in that silvery, dim,
Deep world below, that it seems half-best
To sink into it and there find rest,
Both, both together, ere age can come,
And loving has lost its perfect bloom.
One tilt, dear love, and we both might be
Beyond earth's sorrows eternally.

She. There is something in that; never is love so secure but that there is the menace of change, the shadow of doubt, the fear of something, however vague it be. There is no permanent rising above life's levels. When the wave is at its utmost height, it falls shivered. And then, again, you have expressed that strange, haunting desire, that is almost irrepressible at times, to fling one's self down a precipice on whose edge we stand, or to sink into the depths of some silent, glassy stream over which we are gliding.

Yes, at the height of pleasure comes the longing to stop life there.

He. It is strange how at the very culmination of exalted feeling, when the sensibilities are all alive, fate seems to take a special pleasure in doing them some prosaic violence. How the commonplace and even contemptible facts of life will rush in athwart us in our most poetic moods, and compel us to laugh, despite our annoyance. The lover is just declaring his passion to some trembling girl, for instance, when Bridget opens the door to say, " Please Miss, the butcher says shall he leave a leg of mutton, or will you have a pair of chickens; " — or just as the poet is in the height, let us call it, of his inspiration, some " person from Porlock " will come in on business matters, to try on one's new shoes, perhaps, and the vision of Kubla Khan disappears beyond the horizon of recovery.

She. It is lucky that the " person from Porlock " was anonymous, or hundreds of us would have taken his life.

He. I wonder if he ever existed. It would be just like Coleridge to have invented him as an excuse for his own laziness.

She. Whether he existed or not, he exists no longer, so let us think no more of him, since both he and Coleridge have gone beyond recall, and no one can ever finish that exquisite fragment which he interrupted.

He. Ah! who knows? Martin Farquhar Tupper finished his "Christabel."

She. So he did, in more senses than one, but there are few men so brave as he. What is that you have in your hand now? Read it.

He. Perhaps you won't think it apropos; but here it is: —

Do you remember that most perfect night,
In the full flush of June,
When the wide heavens were tranced in silver light
Of the sad patient moon?
Silent we sat, awed by a strange unrest;
The fathomless, far sky
Our very life absorbed, our thoughts oppressed,
By its immensity.

Lost in that infinite vast, how idle seemed
The best of human speech,

Earth scarcely breathed, so silently she
dreamed,
Save when from some far reach
The faint wind sighed, and stirred the
slumbering trees,
And shadowy stretch and plain
Seemed haunted by unuttered mysteries
Night on its life had lain.

We knew not what we were, or where we
went,
Borne by some unseen power,
Nor in what dream-shaped realms our
spirits spent
That long, yet brief half hour;
I only know that, as a star from high
Slides down the ether thin,
We shot to earth, roused by a startling
cry,
"You 're getting cold — come in."

She. Yes, it always happens so. But why did you say these lines were not apropos to what we were saying?

He. So as not to let you into the secret, and carefully extract the sting of reality from my verses. Confess that you were not at all prepared for its conclusion.

She. I was not, and I can't help thinking it was a little shabby in you so to end it.

He. The world now demands realism, and here you have it.

She. But I don't want it; I have enough of it in life; I don't want it in poetry. I like to have my romantic and ideal world, and to keep it separated from my real and prosaic one.

He. Will this please you better? I have already given you, a little while ago, the longing from below to sink into the deep; here is the longing from above, which may serve as a pendant.

The winds are forever blowing, blowing,
The streams are forever flowing, flowing,
And all things forever going, going,
   Nothing on earth is at rest, —
Ever departing, never abiding,
Sliding away, and onward gliding,
   Alike the worst, the best.

The sky is a glacier paved with snow,
And heaped with many a crowded floe,
And here and there a rift breaks through,
Showing behind an abyss of blue,

A tender silence beyond, afar,
Out of the tumult and rush, and far
Of the winds that drive and rage below,
  And beat on the mountain's crest,
And for all we hope, and more than we know,
  There, perchance, is rest.

She. I am not sure that it is rest we want, but rather security against chance, against the slings and arrows of outrageous fortune, against the irritations of daily life, and the petty needs which crowd about us, mendicants for our time and thoughts. There is nothing we really own. Joy is only lent to us for a moment and then taken away, and over everything broods fear.

He. Since we are in this vein, here is a sonnet to the purpose, and specially for to-day.

Glad is the sunshine, perfect is the day,
A pearl of days, a flawless chrysolite
The sky above us lifts its dome of light,
And loitering clouds along its blue fields stray,
Unshepherded by winds that far away

Are sleeping in their caves. This pure
delight,
This silent, peaceful gladness infinite,
Is troubled by no sorrow, no dismay.
Yes, for o'er all the shadow of a fear
Is brooding, that the restless spirit knows,
The doubting human spirit that forecasts,
Even in the brightest that surrounds us
here,
The inevitable change, — for nought life
knows
Is fixed and permanent, nought lives that
lasts.

She. Very sad, but unfortunately very true. But what is the use of weighing it and pondering it? Let us enjoy Life's beauty as it comes, and not mar it by our melancholy previsions. Take the bitter out of my spirit that you have now infused there, by something a little brighter.

He. I am afraid I have nothing; my portfolio seems suddenly to have gone into mourning. But stop: here is a little trifle, apropos to what you were saying a few moments ago about kissing, which may amuse you. You remember the old Italian proverb, "Un bacio dato non è mai perduto." This is an illustration of it: —

Because we once drove together
  In the moonlight over the snow,
With the sharp bells ringing their tinkling chime,
  So many a year ago,

So, now, as I hear them jingle,
  The winter comes back again,
Though the summer stirs in the heavy trees,
  And the wild rose scents the lane.

We gather our furs around us,
  Our faces the keen air stings,
And noiseless we fly o'er the snow-hushed world
  Almost as if we had wings.

Enough is the joy of mere living,
  Enough is the blood's quick thrill ;
We are simply happy, I care not why,
  We are happy beyond our will.

The trees are with icicles jeweled,
  The walls are o'er-surfed with snow;

The houses with marble whiteness are roofed,
In their windows the home-lights glow.

Through the tense, clear sky above us
The keen stars flash and gleam,
And wrapped in their silent shroud of snow
The broad fields lie and dream.

And jingling with low, sweet clashing
Ring the bells as our good horse goes,
And tossing his head, from his nostrils red
His frosty breath he blows.

And closely you nestle against me,
While around your waist my arm
I have slipped — 't is so bitter, bitter cold —
It is only to keep us warm.

We talk, and then we are silent;
And suddenly — you know why —
I stooped — could I help it ? You lifted your face —
We kissed — there was nobody nigh.

And no one was ever the wiser,
And no one was ever the worse;
The skies did not fall, — as perhaps they ought, —
And we heard no paternal curse.

I never told it — did you, dear? —
From that day unto this;
But my memory keeps in its inmost recess,
Like a perfume, that innocent kiss.

I dare say you have forgotten,
'T was so many a year ago;
Or you may not choose to remember it,
Time may have changed you so.

The world so chills us and kills us,
Perhaps you may scorn to recall
That night, with its innocent impulse, —
Perhaps you 'll deny it all.

But if of that fresh, sweet nature
The veriest vestige survive,
You remember that moment's madness, —
You remember that moonlight drive.

She. I like that.

He. So did I. You see, I always remembered it.

She. Nonsense! You never got it, really.

He. No matter. I remember it. Don't you?

She. I decline to answer. Read me something else — immediately.

He. Here is a little omelette soufflé, not worth serving up. But —

She. Don't make apologies, but read it, — please?

He. Here it is.

I once laughed as loud as the best of them all,
Jenny, my Jenny,
I could foot it as lightly as they at the ball,
Jenny, proud Jenny.
But my foot now is heavy, I wander apart,
And the tears in my eyelids will gather and start;
For, while sweetly you 're smiling
And others beguiling,
Don't you see, my dear Jenny, you 're breaking my heart?

A rosebud she wore in her bonny brown
hair,
Jenny, my Jenny,
When she looked at me first with her
sweet saucy air,
Jenny, dear Jenny,
So red were her lips, and so lithe was her
waist,
That they seemed only made to be kissed
and embraced,
And a sudden, wild madness,
Of longing and gladness,
Thrilled through all my veins with a rap-
turous haste.

There 's Rob, and there 's Bob at her side
that I see,
Jenny, my Jenny,
And she smiles just as sweetly on them
as on me,
Jenny, gay Jenny.
But why should I care ? There are others
as fair
Who will give me their smiles, and their
favors to wear,
And where 's the use sighing
Just like a child crying,
For the jilt of the moon, far away in the
air.

She. The grapes were green.

He. Precisely.

She. But I don't care for that. There 's nothing in it.

He. I did not say there was. I said it might serve as a trifle to take the bitter taste out of your mouth — a punch à la Romaine, with just a little, a very little spirit in it.

She. And why should Jenny have turned her face or her heart to your young man? I have no doubt he was a horrible bore. Why should n't she dance with those pretty fellows Rob and Bob, who were so full of fun and animal spirits, while your young man was mooning about and calling her a jilt, and looking unutterable things into her eyes when he did come near her and trying to press her hand? I have no pity for such fellows. If I had been Jenny I should have turned round on him and said: If you 've got anything to say, for heaven's sake, say it, and have it over. Do you want me — yes? Well, I don't want you. Good-by. I 'm engaged for the next waltz to Bob. I think that would have settled matters.

He. Yes, I should have thought it would. But it did n't.

She. Ah, so she did say so. I like her for it. That is what I call being frank and outspoken. But such fellows will never take no for an answer.

He. No, indeed. She married him at last.

She. What a fool! And I hope was unhappy all her life.

He. I came away at about that time, and cannot tell. — Here is the kind of woman you would like.

She. Now, you are going to read something disagreeable.

He. No. This was a pretty, nice, little iceberg I knew when she was about forty.

Yes! she has lived, lived what she called her life,
  Feebly enjoyed and suffered trivial pain,
Years have slipped by and left no scars of strife
  Upon her little heart and little brain.

No strain or strife of passion has she known;
  Like a pale flower to which no scent is given,

No vivid hues, she in the shade has grown,
Knowing no hell, and worlds away from heaven.

She might have fallen with a richer sense,
But what temptation is she never felt
Cold, pure as snow, was her blank innocence,
So cold, so pure, it knew not how to melt.

She. I beg to ask why you said that was a woman after my mind. Did you mean to insult me?

He. Not at all. I think she is a specimen woman, without a fault. What can you ask more? She never did anything wrong. She was so smooth and cold that vice caromed off from her as one billiard ball from another. What do you accuse her of?

She. I think you once wrote some verses like these: —

As for a heart and soul, my dear,
You have not enough to sin,

Outside so fair, like a peach you are,
With a stone for a heart within.

That 's your idea of a woman. Is it ?

He. I have known such women, who were much admired by your sex, and called noble and pure.

She. And all you men admire the demimonde.

He. And all you women imitate them in their manners, and particularly in their dress.

She. *All* us women ?

He. *All* us men ?

She. There are exceptions.

He. Well, we will be among the exceptions.

She. Have you any other portraits ? They amuse me.

He. Yes, here is one from life:

Ah, yes, you love me, so you say,
But yet a different tale I read,
In those still eyes so cold and gray,
In that ruled brow where lightnings breed,
In those carved lips so set and thin,
That keep their secrets firm within,

O'er which the dazzling smile that gleams,
Keeps flashing like the auroral gleams
Across the still, cold northern sky,
As silently and fitfully.

You say you love me, but I know
'Tis only words you say; no snow
Was ever colder. Just to win
You want, nor would you count it sin,
A heart to break, to gratify
A whim of pride and vanity,
So you might, like an Indian, add
One other scalp to those you had;
Nay! worse, I fear, just for one hour
Of wild caprice, to prove your power,
You would with those cold, quiet eyes,
Ordain my sudden sacrifice.
Smile as you saw me writhe with pain,
And say: Just torture him again,
'T is comical to see him make
Such dreadful faces for my sake.

All this I see and know, and still
My love is all beyond my will.
Take me and torture me, but first
One real, wild, impassioned burst
Of feeling give me. Lift your face,
And let me for a moment's space

Look through those eyes, so calm and
still,
Into your spirit's inmost deeps,
And see, if there within them sleeps
A hidden well of love, a rill
Of living feeling, or — and this
Is what I fear — a dark abyss
Of cold and silent vanity,
Of selfish thought and cruel will, —
That I may love, or turn and flee,
And save myself from all the ill,
The pain, the bliss of loving thee.

She. That is what you might call a charming woman.

He. It is not so very uncommon a woman.

She. Woman? It is a devil, rather.

He. Some women are possessed by the devil of vanity, and have no feelings that are not subordinated to it. When a woman is cruel, she is more cruel than any man. We men can forgive everything to passion; women don't and can't, but men do; but what we cannot pardon is that cold, cruel vanity which is as insatiable as it is heartless. But here, just for a contrast, is another kind of woman, a nice, cheery little person, whom everybody likes, a brook-like little creature.

She. A fool, I suppose, from your preface. You men always like fools.

He. Thanks.

From early light to late at night,
  I chatter, chatter, chatter,
If things are sad or things are bad,
  Dear me ! what does it matter ?
The livelong day to me is gay,
  And I keep always laughing;
The world at best is such a jest,
  'T is only fit for chaffing.

Along the brim of life to skim,
  Not in its depths be sinking,
With jest and smile time to beguile,
  Not bore one's-self with thinking.
To touch and go, and to and fro,
  To gossip, talk, and tattle,
To hear the news, and to amuse
  One's world with endless prattle,

This is my life : I hate all strife,
  With none I am a snarler;
I like to joke with pleasant folk
  In any pleasant parlor.

And when the day has slipped away,
  Ere I blow out my candle,
I sit awhile, and muse and smile,
  O'er that last bit of scandal.

She. Yes, I am afraid, I am afraid there is a little bit of truth in that.

He. A little bit? No more?

She. No, these prattlers have reactions of sadness. We only see the outside, the world-side of them. Be sure that sometimes, out of mere nervousness and over-excitement, they cry as bitterly as at other times they laugh loudly. And besides, this humor is oftentimes put on, just like one's dress, to wear into society. These creatures have the reputation of being gay, and they feel called upon to act up to their reputation; but often when they are alone and the excitement is over, comes a corresponding depression. There is always sadness underlying all humor. There is the old story, you know, of the clown — I forget his name — who nightly provoked the world's laughter in the ring, and who was so depressed and melancholy in his real life and thought, that he consulted a physician to obtain some remedy for his hypochondria. And the physician recommended him to go to hear Grimaldi (that is his name, I remember it now). "Ah," answered he, "I am myself that wretched man."

He. It is possible; but such stories are generally mere inventions. I dare say it bored him to go over the same old jokes nightly, but that is natural. As to his being an extreme hypochondriac, I do not believe it. Besides, his case is different from that of these water-flies that skim and skate over the sunny surface of life. One might as well try to make a cork sink as to depress them. There are characters and temperaments incapable of profound feeling, which cannot be deeply affected by anything, and are as shallow as they are bright. If these persons ever cry it is sympathetically with another, for a moment, but before their tears are dry they are laughing again; and as for this world, they think with Hamlet, though in a different sense, that "there 's nothing serious in it." This is not a vice in them, it proceeds from their own nature. They cannot help it.

She. Yes, I dare say you are right to a

certain extent. But now, read me something else of a different kind.

He. I have two or three love poems. Would you like to hear them ?

She. Yes — perhaps. I am a little tired of love poems.

He. Then we will pass them by.

She. No; on the whole, I will hear them, though there can be little new to say on that subject.

He. Love is always new. It never grows old. It dies when it is young.

She. Not real love. What you men call love, which for the most part is a matter of the senses, may; but what we women mean by love, which is a matter of sentiment and feeling, is very long-lived.

He. Ah ? I did not know that sentiment and feeling belonged only to your sex. I think you also, sometimes, love for a moment. Listen to what a man says on this subject ; not I, of course, — I know your love lasts forever, — but that fellow X., who is a disbeliever — or who was, for a moment — and I call the poem, therefore, "A Moment."

How long would you love me? A lifetime? Ah, that is too long; let us say
A moment. Life's best 's but a moment, and life itself scarcely a day.

Perhaps you might love me that moment; perhaps, while you quaffed
From life's brimming cup, with your sweet face turned up, love's exquisite draught;

All the spirit insatiate thirsting its sweetness to drain,
And a hurry of rapture swift rushing through heart and through brain;

All being condensed to a drop, all the soul, all the sense,
Interfused as by fire, intermingled and throbbing with passion intense;

Just one moment of Life's culmination, its waves' utmost height,
While it lifts its green cavern of opal all sun-fringed, in quivering light;—

Its foam-rose that topples and spreads at the crest of the Fountain's full stress,

That the impulse that lifts cannot hold,
that dies of its very excess ;

Just one rapturous moment, while love
you inhaled like the soul of a flower,
For a breath space, an indrawing breath
space, that words have no power

At their best to express, so divine, so enchanting, its soul-piercing scent,
Thrilling through all the nerves, but at
last in a sigh to be breathed out and
spent;

Just one moment, no longer; and then, all
the strength and desire
Faded out, all the passion exhausted,
naught left of the fire

But the sullen, gray, desolate ashes, — oh,
then, would you cling to me ? Say,
Would you love me, or hate me, or scorn
me, and ruthlessly fling me away ?

Who knows ? Love and hate are so near,
joy and pain, ice and fire, hope and
fear,
That I doubt, the next moment, *this* moment so tender, so perfect, so dear.

This maddening moment I know, let the
next what it chooses reveal;
'T is enough that you love me this moment, let Fate, as she will, spin her
wheel,

Weave her web, cast her net, unto grief
or despair make us prey;
This is mine, this is ours, and, once given,
can never be taken away.

What though, from our dream when we
wake, our love a mere folly may
seem?
What is life at the best but a sleep?
what is love but a dream?

She. I should like to hear her answer to all this rigmarole.

He. You are complimentary.

She. I have no doubt it ended by his love being for a moment and hers for a lifetime, — long after he had forgotten her.

He. No: they were married and settled down, and lived together like very peaceable, good people; and when he was sixty years old he wrote her another poem, of a very different kind. You see, love looks differently from the point of view of sixty years, after forty years of marriage, from what it did at twenty, before marriage.

She. You don't happen to have that last poem, do you? I suppose it was a cold-hearted kind of thing.

He. Yes, it was not in the same key. It was a little toned down. There was not so much clashing of cymbals and blare of brass trumpets in the orchestra. The noisy instruments had all gone away, the gas and footlights were all extinguished, and the piece was played on a summer afternoon by a violin and a violoncello accompanied by an old spinet, while a childish flute lisped on now and then, as if from Arcadian woods.

She. I like that better. Let me hear what they played.

He. It was not a symphony; only a little old song; and here it is: —

Yes, dear, I remember those old days,
  And oh, how charming they were!
I doubt — no, I know that no others to come
  Will ever such feelings stir.

We had only been married a few months,
And love, like a delicate haze,
Veiled in beauty the trivial doings,
The commonest facts of those days.

Life was all smiling before us,
And nature was smiling around;
Spring hovering near us caressed us,
And joy with its aureole crowned;
'Mid the flowers and the trees in blossom,
Afar from the world we dwelt,
And the air was sweet with a thousand odors,
And the world like a full rose smelt.

In the morning I used to leave you,
And that was the only pain; —
Through the grass with its dewdrops diamonded
We walked down the shadowy lane,
And as far as the gate you went with me,
And there, with a kiss we said
Good-by; and you lingering watched me,
And smiled and nodded your head,

And waved your handkerchief to me,
And I constantly turned to see
If you still were there, and my daily work
Seemed a cruel necessity;

The last turn took you away from me,
As on to my task I went,
But your face all day looked up from the page,
As over my book I bent.

And when day was over, how gladly
I rushed from the dusty town!
As I opened the gate, I whistled,
And there was your fluttering gown
As you ran with a smile to meet me,
With your brown curls tossing free,
And your arms were thrown about my neck
As I clasped you close to me.

And the birds broke into a chorus
Of twittering joy and love,
And the golden sunset flamed in the trees,
And gladdened the sky above,
As up the lane together
We slowly loitered along,
While love in our hearts was singing
Its young and exquisite song.

The blood through our veins ran swiftly,
Like a stream of lambent fire;

Our thoughts were all winged, and our spirits
  Uplifted with sweet desire.
My joy, my love, my darling,
  You made the whole world sweet,
And the very ground seemed beautiful
  That you pressed beneath your feet.

What was there more to ask for,
  As I held you closely there,
And you smiled with those gentle, tender eyes,
  And I breathed the scent of your hair?
Stop Time, and speed no further!
  Nothing, as long as we live,
Can give such a radiance of delight,
  As one hour of love can give.

The lilacs were filling with fragrance
  The air along the lane,
And I never smell the lilacs
  But those hours revive again;
And oft, though long years have vanished,
  One whiff of their scent will bring
Those old dear days, with their thrill of life,
  When love was in blossoming.

Time has gone on despite us,
  We both have grown old and gray,
And love itself has grown old and staid,
  But it never has flown away;
The fragile and scented blossom
  Of springtime and youth is shed,
But its sound, sweet fruit of a large content
  Hath ripened for us instead.

She. Ah, well! There was life in the old man still. I think that is more to my taste than the other. There is something more real about it. The other has too many banners flying and gonfalons flouting the air, and there is too much glimmer and glamour about it. This is more like a true experience. Only, one never can tell whether a poet's poetic existence and feeling has any true relation to his own real life.

He. That depends on what you call his real life.

She. For the most part, they give all their sentiment and feeling to their ideal creations, and have very little to spare for their wives. I don't believe much in literary husbands.

He. Nor I. Do you in literary wives?

She. Not I. I suppose, to you, dramatically speaking, one of these poems is just as true to life as the other.

He. Yes, of course, one may be better than the other; but while I was writing them, both seemed equally true. It is all a matter of seeming. A poet, if he is really a poet in the high sense, is transported into situations and personages utterly independent of himself, and, for the time, is more affected by their imaginary experiences and conditions and feelings than by any real experiences of his own.

She. Some poets; not all.

He. I mean, of course, dramatic poets, not didactic. I should be very sorry to be taken literally in many things I write; but it pleases me to imagine myself to be different persons, and to express in my poor way what comes to me as belonging to that person in the supposed situation. In fact, while I write I am that person; as Salvini to-night is Othello, and to-morrow Saul, or Hamlet, or anybody else, all of whom are quite apart from him. But I am getting egotistic.

She. No matter. I excuse you. Men like to be egotistic, and women like them to be so, sometimes, and in some ways. There is a sort of implied compliment in such conversation, when it does not go too far.

He. Then don't let me go too far.

She. Never fear! I will stop you in time. You say that these poems seem equally good to you while you are writing them.

He. I did not say they seemed equally good, but equally true to the person whose character I was assuming. Of course every one, while he is writing, has a certain consciousness that he is doing better or worse, and that the expression he is giving to his thought or feeling is more or less happy and fresh, or the reverse. In some moods we are, so to speak, better conductors of the influence which inspires our work, but that influence itself is beyond our control, and will not respond to our beck and call. Any one who has acquired facility in writing can always, to a certain extent, command his powers, and write, as it were, to order. But we are not absolute masters of our moods, and our faculties at times, despite the spur and whip, work unwillingly and like drudges; while at other times they carry us along freely and gladly, and we feel that we are at the height of our speed. True poems are not written willfully. Our thoughts and even our expressions come to us we know not how or whence. The mind conceives as the body does, without our conscious will. But all its children are not equally fair and well-proportioned. Sometimes the birth is a monster, very rarely an angel, and generally a very human kind of a thing, with many defects and imperfections ; though, whatever it be, it always has a special charm and attraction for the parent.

She. Yes, and the uglier it is the more the parent dotes on it. If I were to attack what you know to be your worst poem, you would be sure at the least to apologize for it and plead for it, or else insist that it was perhaps (you might go so far as to say perhaps) your best.

He. I might, for I do not think any author is the best judge of the relative value of his works.

She. Who is, then ?

He. Posterity, — after the fashion of the time is passed. There are many shapely arrangements of rags and tags which, when new, seem to contain beneath them living creatures, but after they are defaced or shredded and rotted away by time are found to cover nothing but wooden and lifeless frames.

She. Time makes sad havoc even with the best of us, and strips from many a poet much of his fine draperies of verse and singing clothes that so delighted the world in his generation. I suppose we ought only to admire what has stood the test of Time; but what matters it what we like, provided we really like something? The great thing is to enjoy what we have, without waiting for posterity. Besides, however we wait, we never shall overtake posterity, and meantime we may go hungering and thirsting and empty because of our fastidiousness. We can love persons who are not perfect; why not things? Oh, I do so hate critics who are always finding faults and expecting perfection. To hear them talk one would think them superior to all the world; and yet I don't know that their poems and writings are any better than the works they attack so bitterly.

He. I like them better when they are criticising the works of other men than when they fall foul of mine.

She. Well, I will be a gentle critic, if you will read me something more.

He. But I wish you to be honest.

She. I will be as honest as I can be consistently with being friendly; but friendship interferes terribly with honesty.

He. I wonder whether you would like this, which I call "Nina and her Treasures." Nina is a little peasant girl in Tuscany, whom I don't know, whose lover has been faithless, and she is looking over the little trinkets he gave her.

Life, since you left me, love, has been but
 a trouble and pain,
I am always longing and praying to see
 your dear face again.

Fate has been cruel and hard, and so
 many tears I have shed;
The heart is an empty nest for the rain,
 when love has fled.

I am weary, so weary, of life, and the
bitterest pang of all
Is to lie and think of the past, that nothing can ever recall;

To lie in the dark, and think and sob to
myself alone,
Quietly, lest I should waken and grieve
mamma with my moan.

Sometimes I stretch myself out, and think,
as I lie on my bed,
Thus it will be with me, when I 'm laid
out stiff and dead.

Stay not away, O Death! Come soon
and give me my rest,
With the calm lids over my eyes and my
arms crossed over my breast.

Then perhaps he will come, and, gazing
upon me, say,
Nina was good, and our love was an hour
of a summer's day.

Ah, yes, a day that the clouds overcast,
ere the morning was done,
And whose noon was a dreary rain, with
never a glimpse of sun.

If he should stoop and kiss my lips, oh, if I were dead,
I think I should start to life, and rise up in my bed.

But what is the use of thinking, with all this work to do?
Oh, yes, mamma, I hear you; I 'll come in a moment to you.

What am I doing? Nothing. I 'm putting some things away;
No, — not the trinkets of Gigi. (Madonna, forgive me, I pray!)

Oh, no; you never will throw them into the river, I know.
Just wait till I find my needle, and then I 'll come in and sew.

Oh, this is the hardest of all, — to smile and to chatter lies,
While my heart is breaking and tears blind everything to my eyes.

When will there come an end, Madonna mia, — I say,
When will there come an end, and the whole world pass away?

She. Poor little Nina! I feel quite sad about her. Did he ever come back?

He. No; Nina married another fellow, who owned a cow and had a thousand francs for a fortune, and — but I 'll tell you her story another time.

She. So Nina was a real person?

He. Not in the least; but she might have been.

She. I think for the present we have had enough of love; now read me something of a different kind.

He. No, I must read you one more poem about love, as expressing the way a man takes his disappointment, just in contrast to Nina. You have set me going on this track, and I must take one step more, and then we will close the book. I call it

A BLACK DAY.

I thought it was dead;
That the years had crushed it down and trodden it out
With their cruel tramp and tread;
That nothing was left but the ashes, cold and gray,
Of a love that had wholly passed away,

With its hope, and fear, and joy, and doubt.
But nothing utterly dies;
And again, as I tread the paths of these silent woods,
Where we walked and loved a few long years ago,
And list to the wind's soft sighs
Rustling the solitudes,
And the low, perpetual hum and welling flow
Of the torrent that finds its way
And talks to itself among the mossy, gray
And unchanged boulders and stones —
Again, with a sudden, sharp surprise,
The old life leaps anew with a rush before me:
The cloud of these dreary years that have darkened o'er me
Lifts and passes, and you are again beside me:
The tones of your voice I hear; I look in your tender eyes,
And I fiercely and vainly long for what is denied me,
And I curse my cruel fate, as I cursed it then.

Ah! what has brought me here to this fatal glen?
I would that the sky was a globe of fragile glass,
That I to atoms might dash it;
And the flowers, and the trees, and the whole wide world around
Were all at my very feet lying here on the ground,
That I into flinders might pash it.
With a terrible impotent rage my close-clenched hand
I shake at these pitiless skies that glare above,
And the smothered flame of a wild, despairing love,
One breath of the breeze with a sudden strength has fanned
To a world-wide conflagration;
And I cry in a torture of pain,
With a cry that is all in vain,
Come back, come back again,
And deny me not in my desperation
The love that I crave, — the love you denied of yore!
Come back and behold me, and into my spirit pour
Some balm of consolation;

Or strike me dead to the earth, that I no
more
May grovel, tortured in spirit and wild
with grief,
Looking out all over the world in vain for
relief.
Come back, I implore!

Curses upon the place, the time, the
hour,
When first I met you;
Curses upon myself, that am all without
the power,
Despite my will, to forget you!
Ah, would to God that you for an hour's
brief space —
Only an hour — might suffer as I do!
Ah, would to God that you were here
in my place,
With the barb in your heart, like a deer
at the end of the race,
With naught but despair beside you,
Nothing but death and the heartless skies
above,
That laugh alike at our joy and our grief
and our love.

But no! ah no! you are happy and gay,
and glad.

And what care you for the memories dark and sad
  That have ruined my hereafter.
Brook-like, above my broken hopes that lie
Hidden perchance beneath your memory,
  Your light thoughts run with laughter.
I see you smiling, — I know you are smiling still;
At the fountain of joy you stoop and drink your fill,
  Careless whose heart you are breaking.
But the terrible thirst with which I am curst,
  Ah me ! is beyond all slaking;
For the stream of which I am drinking
Is a torrent of fire and fierce desire.
For me there is no more thinking,
No more hoping, or dreaming, or yearning,
No more living, and no more laughing,
Nothing for me but that fountain burning,
Where my spirit is ever quaffing.

Curses upon the hour and the place, I say!
Why did my footsteps lead me here ?
Will these wild memories never pass away ?

Can I never forget you? Ah, too dear,
too dear!
Never while life shall last,
Never, ah never, till all the world has
passed!

She. That is not what I should call a nice young man. I do not at all approve of him.

He. Poor fellow! He blew his brains out, a week after, on that same spot. It is a curious fact that women never do this, — and yet they are always talking of dying for love.

She. They have too much sense to do such stupid things. They embroider their disappointments into tidies and chair backs and table covers, which is far more sensible, or net it away into purses and shawls and bedquilts.

He. It is time for us to be going. Shall we stroll along?

She. No! One more poem.

He. No, no! I have already read you too many of these scraps, which after all are not worth reading; and besides, the day is going. Let us pass the rest of it without reading. Let us wander along together through this glen.

She. No. I must finish embroidering this flower first. It will scarcely take me a quarter of an hour, and you must now read me one more poem; and let it be a serious one, — one of your best.

He. I don't know what is best, and what is worst. But if you want a serious one, I will read you this. It is a lost ode of Horace addressed to Victor. You will not find it in his printed works. I discovered it in an old Palimpsest MS., and translated it word for word.

TO VICTOR.

Nor I, nor thou, with all our seeking, know
Whither, when life is over, we shall go,
Nor what awaits us on that farther shore,
Hid from our eyes by Acheron's dark flow.

We only know — and this we must endure —
That Death waits for us, whom no prayer or lure
Can move or change; towards whose outstretched arms
Each moment onward drives us, silent, sure.

What he conceals behind that veil he draws
We know not, Victor; but his shadow awes
This life of ours, and in the very height
Of joy and love he bids us shuddering pause.

Virtue avails us not, nor wealth, nor power,
To stay one moment the appointed hour.
Marcellus, Cæsar, Virgil, all have gone, —
The fatal sickle reaps grain, bud, and flower.

Where are they now? Upon some unknown strand
Shall we again behold them, clasp their hand,
And, untormented by the ills of life,
Renew our friendship, and together stand?

Or, when the end is reached, — and come it must, —
Shall we, despite the hope in which we trust,

Feel nothing more, nor love, nor joy,
nor pain,
But be at last mere mute, insensate dust?
If so, then virtue is a lying snare.
Let us fill high the bowl, drown sullen
care,
Reap the earth's joys and all the joys
of sense,
And of Life's bounty seize our fullest
share.

The Gods forbid the curious human eye
Into the Future's mystery to spy.
They give us hour by hour, and scarcely
that;
For, ere the hour is measured, we may die.

But if thou goest before me where no
speech,
No word of friendship, no warm grasp,
can reach,
Let me not linger. May the pitying
Gods
Send the same final summons unto each!

Whether stern Death reach out his hand
to bless
Or sweep us down to blank, dire nothing-
ness —

Whate'er may come, together let us go
Where, at the worst, we shall escape life's
stress.

She. Ah, yes; that is serious enough, and sad enough. What have we learned since Horace? How much nearer are we to the solving of the eternal riddle that ever is taunting us? What do we know of anything?

He. *Que sçais-je?* You know Montaigne's motto. That is the question one always asks.

She. And the answer is?

He. *Rien.* It is perfectly simple.

She. Then what is the use of it all? To what purpose are all our struggles, all our yearnings, all our failures, all our defeats, since life always at the last ends in defeat?

He. That depends on what you mean by defeat. It is not always the conquerors who triumph. To act well one's part is the triumph. That is the old stoic doctrine so fully illustrated in the life and meditations of Marcus Aurelius. Act according to your nature, he says. That is what life requires of you. Develop your noble and aspiring principles as the tree does, which grows up to the sun and the sky, and bears its fruit without triumph, and drops it without regret, and gathers its joy out of heaven, seeking not to bear the fruit which does not belong to it. Even the imperfect has its exquisite charm, as the sweetest figs have their rinds torn and scratched. It is not the smooth which is the best. The trials of life have an infinite value. And now to hear the end of the whole matter, let me read for you my very last, — a pæan for the conquered, an Io Victis: —

IO VICTIS!

I SING the hymn of the conquered, who fell in the Battle of Life, —
The hymn of the wounded, the beaten, who died overwhelmed in the strife;
Not the jubilant song of the victors, for whom the resounding acclaim
Of nations was lifted in chorus, whose brows wore the chaplet of fame,
But the hymn of the low and the humble, the weary, the broken in heart,
Who strove and who failed, acting bravely a silent and desperate part;

Whose youth bore no flower on its
branches, whose hopes burned in
ashes away,
From whose hands slipped the prize they
had grasped at, who stood at the
dying of day
With the wreck of their life all around
them, unpitied, unheeded, alone,
With Death swooping down o'er their
failure, and all but their faith
overthrown.

While the voice of the world shouts its
chorus, — its pæan for those who
have won;
While the trumpet is sounding triumph-
ant, and high to the breeze and
the sun
Glad banners are waving, hands clapping,
and hurrying feet
Thronging after the laurel-crowned vic-
tors, I stand on the field of de-
feat,
In the shadow, with those who are fallen,
and wounded, and dying, and
there
Chant a requiem low, place my hand on
their pain-knotted brows, breathe
a prayer,

Hold the hand that is helpless, and whisper, "They only the victory win,

Who have fought the good fight, and have vanquished the demon that tempts us within;
Who have held to their faith unseduced by the prize that the world holds on high;
Who have dared for a high cause to suffer, resist, fight, — if need be, to die."

Speak, History! who are Life's victors? Unroll thy long annals, and say,
Are they those whom the world called the victors — who won the success of a day?
The martyrs, or Nero? The Spartans, who fell at Thermopylæ's tryst,
Or the Persians and Xerxes? His judges or Socrates? Pilate or Christ?

She. Thank you. That is a consolation to us who do not win the laurel.

The poem he was then scribbling when

she interrupted him, he did not read. But he afterwards sent it to her, and as it describes the glen where the conversation took place, it may as well be added to those he really read.

IN THE GLEN.

HERE in this cool, secluded glen
Alone with Nature let me lie,
Where no rude voice or peering eyes of men
Disturbs its perfect peace and privacy;
Where through the swaying firs the restless breeze
Sighs softly and the murmuring torrent flows,
Singing the same low song as on it goes,
That it hath sung for countless centuries;
Now welling through the mossy rocks, now spilled
In little sparkling falls, now lingering, stilled,
In brown, deep pools to hold the mirrored skies,
As brown, as clear, as some fair maiden's eyes,
And filled like them with silent mysteries.

One side the shelving slopes, through
which its song
The torrent sings, the firs' tall columns
throng,
Spreading their dark green tops against
the blue ;
And on the brown, fine carpet at their
feet
Long strips and flecks of sun strike glim-
mering through,
Where gleaming specks of insects
through them fleet.
Along the other slope green beeches spread
Their spotted canopy of light and shade,
And on the brown, transparent stream
below
Their quivering, tessellated pavement
throw.

Here ferns and bracken spread their
plumy spray ;
Here the wild rose gropes out against the
gray
Moss-cushioned rocks, and o'er the torrent
swings ;
Here o'er the bank the sombre ivy strings,
And the scorned thistle bears its royal
crown ;

Here wild clematis stretches, wavering
down ;
And, 'mid a mass of tangled weeds that
know
Scarcely a name, and all neglected grow,
A tribe of gracious flowers peeps smiling
up :
The humble dandelion, buttercup,
And spindled gorse here show their gleam-
ing gold ;
The bright-eyed daisy, innocently bold,
Stars the lush green ; the purple malva
lifts
Its spreading cup. From tufted black-
berries drifts
A snow of blossoms, scenting with their
breath
The summer air ; and, sacred to St. John,
The magic flower that maidens cull at
dawn ;
And blue forgot-me-nots, scarce seen be-
neath
The feathery grass ; and the white hem-
lock's face ;
And all the wild, untrained, and happy
race
Of Nature's children, through whose
blooms the bees,
Busy for honey hovering, hum and tease.

Softened, by distance, from the woods
remote,
Rings, now and then, the blackbird's li-
quid note ;
Or the jay scolds, or far up in the sky
Trills out the lark's long, quivering mel-
ody ;
Or, its melodious passion pouring out,
In the green shadow hid, the nightingale
Stills all the world to listen to its tale,
The same sweet tale that centuries past it
sung
To Grecian ears, when Poesy was young ;
Or the glad goldfinch tunes his tremulous
throat,
Or with a sudden chirp some linnet gray
Darts up the gorge, to drink at these cool
springs,
And at a glimpse of me flits swift away.

A faint, fine hum of myriad quivering
wings
Fills all the air ; the idle butterfly
Drifts down the glen ; and through the
grasses low
Creep swarms of busy creatures to and
fro,
And have their loves, and joys, and strife
and hate,

Intent upon a life to us unknown.
On the o'erhanging bowlders glance and gleam
Quick, quivering lights reflected from the stream,
Where water-spiders poise and darting skate,
Their shadows on its dappled sand-floor thrown.
Across the bowlders bare and pine-slopes brown,
Like dials of the day that passes by,
The firs' long shadow-index silently,
So silently, is ever stealing on,
We scarcely heed the unpausing race of time
So swift and noiseless ; and some subtle spell
Seems to have lulled to sleep this shadowy dell,
As if it lay in some enchanted clime,
Haunted by dreams that never poet's rhyme
Nor music's voice to waking ears can tell.

All is so peaceful here that weary thought
Half falls asleep, nor seeks to find the key
Of the pervading, unsolved mystery

Through which we move, by which our
life is wrought.
Here, magnetized by Nature, if the eye
Upglancing should discern in the soft
shade
Some Dryad's form, or, where the waters
braid
Their silvery windings, haply should
descry
Some naked Naiad leaning on the rocks,
Her feet dropped in its basin, while her
locks
She lifts from off her shoulders unafraid,
And gazes round, or looks into the cool
Tranced mirror of the softly-gleaming
pool,
To see her polished limbs and bosom bare
And sweet, dim eyes and smile reflected
there,
'T would scarce seem strange, but only as
it were
A natural presence, natural as yon rose
That spreads its beauty careless to the air,
And knows not whence it came nor why
it grows,
And just as simply, innocently there ;
The sweet presiding spirit of some tree,
The soul indwelling in the murmuring
brook,

Whose voice we hear, whose form we cannot see,
On whom, at last, 't is given us to look;
As if dear Nature for a moment's space
Lifted her veil and met us face to face.

Such Grecian thought is false to our rude sense,
That naught believes, or feels, or hears, or sees
Of what the world in happier days of Greece
Felt with a feeling gentle and intense.
We are divorced from Nature; our dull ears
Catch not the music of the finer spheres,
See not the spirits that in Nature dwell
In leafy groves through which they glancing look,
In the dim music of the singing brook,
And lurk half hidden and half audible.
To us the world is dead. The soul of things,
The life that haunts us with imaginings,
That lives, breathes, throbs in all we hear and see,
The charm, the secret hidden everywhere,
Evades all reason, spurns philosophy,

And scorns by boasting science to be
tracked.
Hunt as we will all matter to the end,
Life flits before it ; last, as first, we find
Naught but dead structure and the dust
of fact ;
The infinite gap we cannot apprehend,
The somewhat that is life — the inform-
ing mind.

Even here in this still glen I cannot flee
The secret that torments us everywhere.
In cloud, sky, rock, tree, man, its mystery
Pursues us ever to the same despair.
What says this brook, that ever murmur-
ing flows ?
What whisper these tall trees that talk
alway ?
What secret hides the perfume of this
rose ?
What is it that dear Nature strives to
say ?
Our sense is dull, we cannot understand
The voice we hear — but, oh ! so far away
As from a world beyond our night and
day,
A dream-voice from some dim, imagined
land.

Here dreaming on in idle, tranquil mood,
Lulled by the tune that Nature softly
plays,
Our wandering thoughts, by some strange
spell subdued,
Are calmed and stilled, and all seems
sweet and good,
And she our mother seems, that on her
breast,
With murmuring voice, and gentle, whis-
pering ways,
Hushes her child within her arms to rest;
And, though the child scarce knoweth
what she says,
He feels her presence gently o'er him
brood.

And yet, O Nature, thou no mother art,
But for a moment, like to this, at best
A stern step-mother thou, that to thy heart
Claspest thy child by some caprice pos-
sessed,
Then, careless of his fate, abandonest,
Flinging him off from thee to wail and cry,
All heedless if he live or if he die.
Is it for us thou, reckless, squanderest
Thy beauty with such wide and lavish
waste?

For us? Ah! no; were we all swept
away,
What wouldst thou care? No change
upon thy face
Would answer to our sorrow or disgrace,
Alike to those who love, laugh, weep, or
pray.
Glares not the sun impertinent upon
Our darkest griefs? Do not the glad
flowers blow,
The unpausing hours, days, seasons come
and go,
Despite our joys and loves? To all our
woe
Have we a sympathetic answer ever
won?
Are thy stones softer on the path we
tread
Because our thoughts are journeying with
the dead?
Is not this world, with all its beauty, rife
With endless war, death preying upon
life,
Perpetual horror, pain, crime, discord,
strife,
Night chasing day, storms driving sun-
shine out?
And yet through all impassive, stern, and
cold,

With folded hands, which hide whate'er
they hold,
Like Nemesis, thou standest, speaking
not,
Before the gates of Fate ; and, if they
ope,
To show one glimpse beyond, one gleam
of hope,
'T is but an instant; then the door is
shut ;
And, poor, blind creatures, here astray
we grope,
Stretching our hands out where we can-
not see,
Through the dark paths of this world's
mystery.

And yet, why spoil the day with thoughts
like these ?
Better to lie beneath these whispering
trees
And take the joy the moment gives, and
feel
The glad, pure day, the gently lifting
breeze
That steals their odors from the uncon-
scious flowers,
Nor seek what Nature never will reveal,

The hidden secret of our destinies.
Let it all go — whate'er it is it is,
And, come what will, this day, at least, is
ours.
My hour is gone, dear glen, and now
farewell.
Here you the self-same song, bright
brook, will sing;
Here you, dark firs, the self-same tale
will tell,
Mysterious, to the low wind whispering,
How many a summer day to other ears,
When I am gone, beyond all doubts,
hopes, fears,
Beyond all sights and sounds of this fair
world,
Into the dim beyond; in time to come
Will many a dreamer sit for many an
hour,
Lulled by your murmur, and the insects'
hum,
And many a poet praise you. Clasped
and curled
Beside these rocks, and plucking some
chance flower,
Will many a pair of lovers linger, dumb
With loves too much for utterance, all
too weak

The charm they feel, the joy they own, to
speak.
Here wandering from the noisy city's
maze,
How many an idle, casual visitor
Thy beauty with a careless tone will
praise,
And turn away without one true heart-
stir.
Here the dull woodman, thinking but of
gain,
Heedless of any Dryad's shriek of pain,
Will fell with ringing axe this living
wood ;
And here some gentle child, o'er whom
the dream
And lingering lights of former being
brood,
Perchance may meet some Naiad at this
stream,
By whom her language shall be under-
stood,
And here together they will talk and
play,
And many a secret she will strive to
tell
That here she learns, and all the world
will say,

Laughing : "Dear child, this is not credible."
Ah Heaven! we know so much who nothing know!
Only to children and in poets' ears,
At whom the wise world wondering smiles and sneers,
Secrets of God are whispered here below.
Only to them, and those whose gentle heart
Is opened wide to list for Beauty's call,
Will Nature lean to whisper the least part
Of that great mystery which circles all.
The wise, dull world, with solid facts content,
Laughs at all dreamers, deeming nothing good
Save what is touched, seen, handled, understood.
Well, let it laugh! To me the firmament
Is more than gleaming lights; more than mere wood
These leafy groves; and more these murmuring streams
Than running waters. This wide, vaporous sky,

Painted by morning, fired by sunset
gleams,
These winds that breathe around this
swinging world,
This restless ocean, moaning constantly,
These storms across the shuddering
forests whirled,
The season's still processions, day and
night,
That each the other silently pursues,
Sure and unchanging in their even flight,
And all these changing shows and forms
and hues
Not for mere use were given, nor mere
delight.
Beauty is theirs and power, and, more, a
fine
Dim mystery shrouds them man can ne'er
divine.
Harvests that sweeten life and thought
they bear
Imponderable, exquisite, and rare,
That take the spirit with a sweet sur-
prise.
Dreams haunt them, intimations, prophe-
cies,
Glad lessons, adumbrations, spirit gleams,
That, when the loving heart evokes them,
rise.

Others may reap their solid facts; for
me,
I am content to gather inwardly
Their silent harvest of poetic dreams

www.ingramcontent.com/pod-product-compliance
Lightning Source LLC
LaVergne TN
LVHW021428110826
845150LV00007B/2142

* 9 7 8 1 4 2 5 5 0 6 9 6 4 *